EMMANUEL JOSEPH

Designing a Life of Simplicity, Connection, and Abundance

Copyright © 2025 by Emmanuel Joseph

All rights reserved. No part of this publication may be reproduced, stored or transmitted in any form or by any means, electronic, mechanical, photocopying, recording, scanning, or otherwise without written permission from the publisher. It is illegal to copy this book, post it to a website, or distribute it by any other means without permission.

First edition

This book was professionally typeset on Reedsy.
Find out more at reedsy.com

Contents

1. Chapter 1: Embracing Minimalism — 1
2. Chapter 2: The Power of Mindfulness — 3
3. Chapter 3: Decluttering Your Physical Space — 5
4. Chapter 4: Simplifying Your Schedule — 7
5. Chapter 5: Building Meaningful Connections — 8
6. Chapter 6: Nurturing Self-Care — 9
7. Chapter 7: Cultivating Gratitude — 10
8. Chapter 8: Living with Intention — 11
9. Chapter 9: Financial Simplicity and Abundance — 12
10. Chapter 10: The Joy of Giving — 13
11. Chapter 11: Embracing Change — 14
12. Chapter 12: Finding Balance — 15
13. Chapter 13: Connecting with Nature — 16
14. Chapter 14: Pursuing Passion and Purpose — 17
15. Chapter 15: Cultivating Creativity — 18
16. Chapter 16: Practicing Mindful Consumption — 19
17. Chapter 17: Designing Your Ideal Life — 20

1

Chapter 1: Embracing Minimalism

In our fast-paced, consumption-driven world, minimalism offers a refreshing alternative. By stripping away the excess, we focus on what truly matters. Minimalism isn't just about owning fewer things; it's a mindset that values quality over quantity. It emphasizes intentionality in every aspect of life, from our possessions to our relationships. By embracing minimalism, we create space for more meaningful experiences and connections.

Imagine walking into a room where every item has a purpose and brings you joy. This is the essence of minimalism. It's not about depriving ourselves but about making room for what truly enriches our lives. By clearing out the clutter, we free ourselves from the constant noise and distraction that can overwhelm us. This chapter will explore the philosophy of minimalism and provide practical tips on how to begin this transformative journey.

One way to start is by assessing our current possessions and determining what truly adds value to our lives. This process can be liberating as we let go of items that no longer serve us. It can also be challenging, as we confront the emotional attachments we have to certain belongings. However, the result is a living space that reflects our true selves and supports our well-being.

Additionally, minimalism encourages us to reevaluate our consumption habits. It's about being mindful of what we bring into our lives, whether it's new clothes, gadgets, or even experiences. By prioritizing quality over quantity, we can make more intentional choices that align with our values. Minimalism isn't a one-size-fits-all approach; it's about finding what works best for us and creating a life that is both simple and fulfilling.

2

Chapter 2: The Power of Mindfulness

Mindfulness is the practice of being fully present in the moment. It allows us to appreciate life's simple pleasures and develop a deeper connection with ourselves and others. In a world filled with distractions, mindfulness helps us find peace and clarity. It involves paying attention to our thoughts, emotions, and sensations without judgment. By cultivating mindfulness, we become more aware of our habits and patterns, enabling us to make conscious choices.

Incorporating mindfulness into our daily routine can be transformative. It starts with small practices, such as mindful breathing or mindful eating. These practices encourage us to slow down and savor each moment. Over time, mindfulness can become a way of life, influencing how we interact with others and how we handle stress. This chapter delves into the benefits of mindfulness and offers techniques to incorporate it into daily life.

One technique is mindful meditation, which involves setting aside a few minutes each day to sit quietly and focus on our breath. This practice can help us develop greater awareness of our thoughts and emotions, allowing us to respond to situations with greater clarity and calm. Another technique is mindful walking, which involves paying attention to the sensations of our feet touching the ground and the sights and sounds around us.

Mindfulness also extends to our interactions with others. By being fully present in our conversations and listening deeply, we can build stronger and more meaningful connections. This chapter will provide practical tips for cultivating mindfulness in various aspects of our lives, from our daily routines to our relationships.

3

Chapter 3: Decluttering Your Physical Space

A cluttered environment can contribute to stress and overwhelm. By decluttering our physical space, we create a sense of order and tranquility. This process involves letting go of items that no longer serve us and organizing our belongings in a way that supports our lifestyle. Decluttering goes beyond tidying up; it's about creating a space that reflects our values and priorities.

Imagine walking into a room where everything has its place, and there's a sense of calm and clarity. Decluttering starts with identifying areas in our home that need attention. It could be a messy closet, an overflowing kitchen drawer, or a cluttered workspace. The goal is to tackle one area at a time, sorting through items and deciding what to keep, donate, or discard. This chapter provides practical strategies for decluttering different areas of the home and maintaining a clutter-free environment.

One effective method is the KonMari approach, which involves keeping only items that "spark joy." By focusing on the positive emotions that our belongings evoke, we can make more intentional choices about what to keep. Additionally, implementing organizational systems, such as labeled bins and storage solutions, can help us maintain a tidy space. Decluttering is an ongoing process, and this chapter offers tips for regularly reassessing and maintaining our living space.

4

Chapter 4: Simplifying Your Schedule

Our schedules often become overloaded with commitments and obligations, leaving little room for what truly matters. Simplifying our schedule involves prioritizing activities that align with our values and eliminating or delegating tasks that don't. It's about finding a balance between productivity and rest. By simplifying our schedule, we create time for self-care, hobbies, and meaningful connections.

One way to simplify our schedule is by conducting a time audit. This involves tracking how we spend our time over a week and identifying areas where we can cut back or delegate tasks. It's important to set boundaries and learn to say no to commitments that don't align with our priorities. This chapter offers practical tips for managing time and creating a more intentional daily routine.

Creating a daily or weekly plan can help us stay organized and focused on what matters most. By setting aside dedicated time for important activities, such as exercise, family time, and self-care, we can ensure that our schedule reflects our values. This chapter also explores the benefits of creating a "not-to-do" list, which helps us identify tasks that we can eliminate or delegate.

5

Chapter 5: Building Meaningful Connections

Human connection is essential for our well-being. Building meaningful relationships involves being present, authentic, and empathetic. It's about listening deeply and sharing our true selves with others. In a digital age where superficial interactions are common, cultivating genuine connections requires effort and intentionality.

One way to build meaningful connections is by practicing active listening. This involves giving our full attention to the person we are communicating with and responding thoughtfully. It's important to show empathy and understanding, even if we don't agree with everything being said. This chapter explores the importance of human connection and provides strategies for nurturing and sustaining meaningful relationships.

Another key aspect of building connections is being vulnerable and authentic. By sharing our true thoughts and feelings, we create an environment where others feel comfortable doing the same. This chapter offers tips for building trust and deepening relationships, whether with family, friends, or colleagues.

6

Chapter 6: Nurturing Self-Care

Self-care is the foundation of a fulfilling and abundant life. It involves taking care of our physical, mental, and emotional well-being. Self-care is not a luxury but a necessity. It includes practices such as regular exercise, healthy eating, adequate sleep, and stress management. By prioritizing self-care, we replenish our energy and enhance our overall quality of life.

One way to nurture self-care is by creating a self-care routine that includes activities that bring us joy and relaxation. This could involve practicing yoga, journaling, or spending time in nature. It's important to listen to our bodies and give ourselves permission to rest and recharge. This chapter discusses the importance of self-care and offers practical tips for incorporating it into daily routines.

Additionally, self-care involves setting boundaries and learning to say no to activities that drain our energy. It's important to recognize our limits and prioritize our well-being. This chapter explores the benefits of self-care and provides strategies for creating a balanced and fulfilling life.

7

Chapter 7: Cultivating Gratitude

Gratitude is a powerful practice that shifts our focus from what we lack to what we have. It involves recognizing and appreciating the positive aspects of our lives, no matter how small. Gratitude fosters a sense of abundance and contentment. It helps us develop a positive outlook and strengthens our resilience in the face of challenges.

One way to cultivate gratitude is by keeping a gratitude journal. This involves writing down a few things we are grateful for each day. It can be as simple as appreciating a sunny day, a kind gesture from a friend, or a delicious meal. By regularly reflecting on the good things in our lives, we train our minds to focus on positivity. This chapter explores the benefits of gratitude and offers techniques for cultivating a grateful mindset.

Another practice is expressing gratitude to others. This can be done through a heartfelt note, a genuine compliment, or simply saying thank you. By acknowledging the contributions of others, we strengthen our relationships and create a culture of appreciation. This chapter provides practical tips for incorporating gratitude into daily life.

8

Chapter 8: Living with Intention

Living with intention means making conscious choices that align with our values and goals. It's about being deliberate in our actions and decisions. By living with intention, we create a life that is meaningful and fulfilling.

One way to live with intention is by setting clear goals and priorities. This involves reflecting on what truly matters to us and making decisions that support those priorities. It's important to regularly reassess our goals and adjust our actions accordingly. This chapter discusses the importance of setting intentions and offers practical strategies for aligning daily actions with long-term goals.

Another aspect of intentional living is being mindful of our habits and routines. By identifying habits that no longer serve us and replacing them with more positive behaviors, we can create a more intentional and fulfilling life. This chapter provides tips for developing and maintaining intentional habits.

9

Chapter 9: Financial Simplicity and Abundance

Financial simplicity involves managing our finances in a way that supports our values and goals. It's about living within our means, reducing debt, and saving for the future. Financial abundance is not about accumulating wealth but achieving financial freedom and security.

One way to achieve financial simplicity is by creating a budget that reflects our priorities. This involves tracking our income and expenses and identifying areas where we can cut back. It's important to differentiate between needs and wants and make mindful spending decisions. This chapter provides practical tips for budgeting, saving, and making mindful financial decisions.

Another aspect of financial simplicity is reducing debt. This can be achieved by creating a debt repayment plan and prioritizing high-interest debts. By reducing our debt, we create financial freedom and reduce stress. This chapter explores strategies for managing debt and achieving financial abundance.

10

Chapter 10: The Joy of Giving

Giving brings joy and fulfillment. It's about sharing our time, resources, and talents with others. Generosity creates a sense of connection and contributes to our overall well-being.

One way to experience the joy of giving is by volunteering. This involves offering our time and skills to support a cause we care about. Volunteering not only benefits others but also gives us a sense of purpose and fulfillment. This chapter explores the benefits of giving and provides ideas for incorporating acts of kindness and generosity into daily life.

Another way to give is through charitable donations. By supporting organizations that align with our values, we can make a positive impact on the world. This chapter offers practical tips for mindful giving and creating a culture of generosity.

11

Chapter 11: Embracing Change

Change is an inevitable part of life. Embracing change involves being open to new experiences and opportunities. It's about adapting to challenges and viewing them as growth opportunities.

One way to embrace change is by cultivating a mindset of resilience. This involves recognizing that change is a natural part of life and that we have the strength and resources to navigate it. By viewing challenges as opportunities for growth, we can approach change with a positive attitude. This chapter discusses the importance of resilience and offers strategies for navigating change with grace and positivity.

Another aspect of embracing change is being open to new experiences. This can involve stepping out of our comfort zones and trying new activities or pursuing new interests. By being open to change, we can discover new passions and opportunities. This chapter provides practical tips for developing a mindset of openness and adaptability.

12

Chapter 12: Finding Balance

Balance is essential for a harmonious and fulfilling life. It's about creating equilibrium between work, play, rest, and relationships. Finding balance requires self-awareness and the ability to set boundaries.

One way to find balance is by setting priorities and allocating time for activities that matter most. This involves recognizing our limits and ensuring that we have time for rest and relaxation. It's important to set boundaries and say no to commitments that don't align with our priorities. This chapter explores the importance of balance and offers practical tips for achieving it in various aspects of life.

Another aspect of balance is creating a daily routine that includes time for work, play, and rest. By establishing a routine that reflects our values and priorities, we can create a more balanced and fulfilling life. This chapter provides tips for creating and maintaining a balanced daily routine.

13

Chapter 13: Connecting with Nature

Nature has a profound impact on our well-being. Connecting with nature involves spending time outdoors and appreciating the natural world. It helps us feel grounded, reduces stress, and enhances our overall health.

One way to connect with nature is by incorporating outdoor activities into our daily routine. This could involve taking a walk in the park, gardening, or simply sitting outside and enjoying the fresh air. By spending time in nature, we can recharge and find a sense of peace and tranquility. This chapter discusses the benefits of nature connection and provides ideas for incorporating nature into daily life.

Another aspect of connecting with nature is practicing mindfulness while outdoors. This involves paying attention to the sights, sounds, and sensations of the natural world. By being fully present in nature, we can develop a deeper appreciation for its beauty and wonder. This chapter offers practical tips for cultivating mindfulness in nature.

14

Chapter 14: Pursuing Passion and Purpose

Passion and purpose give our lives meaning and direction. Pursuing our passions involves engaging in activities that bring us joy and fulfillment. It's about following our interests and talents. Living with purpose means contributing to something larger than ourselves.

One way to pursue passion and purpose is by identifying our interests and talents. This involves reflecting on what activities bring us joy and fulfillment and finding ways to incorporate them into our lives. By pursuing our passions, we can create a more meaningful and fulfilling life. This chapter explores the importance of passion and purpose and offers strategies for discovering and pursuing them.

Another aspect of living with purpose is contributing to something larger than ourselves. This could involve volunteering, supporting a cause we care about, or pursuing a career that aligns with our values. By living with purpose, we can create a positive impact on the world and find greater fulfillment. This chapter provides practical tips for living with passion and purpose.

15

Chapter 15: Cultivating Creativity

Creativity enriches our lives and fosters a sense of playfulness and curiosity. It's about exploring new ideas, expressing ourselves, and thinking outside the box. Cultivating creativity involves embracing imperfections and taking risks.

One way to cultivate creativity is by engaging in creative activities regularly. This could involve painting, writing, cooking, or any other activity that allows us to express ourselves. It's important to approach these activities with an open mind and a willingness to experiment. This chapter discusses the benefits of creativity and offers practical tips for nurturing creative expression.

Another aspect of cultivating creativity is being open to new experiences and perspectives. By exposing ourselves to different cultures, ideas, and art forms, we can expand our creative horizons. This chapter provides tips for finding inspiration and staying curious.

16

Chapter 16: Practicing Mindful Consumption

Mindful consumption involves being intentional about what we buy and consume. It's about making choices that align with our values and support sustainable living. Mindful consumption reduces waste and promotes a simpler and more eco-friendly lifestyle.

One way to practice mindful consumption is by evaluating our purchasing habits. This involves considering whether an item is truly necessary and aligns with our values before making a purchase. By prioritizing quality over quantity, we can make more intentional and sustainable choices. This chapter provides practical tips for adopting mindful consumption habits.

Another aspect of mindful consumption is reducing waste. This can involve practices such as recycling, composting, and reducing single-use items. By being mindful of our environmental impact, we can contribute to a healthier planet. This chapter explores the benefits of mindful consumption and offers strategies for reducing waste.

17

Chapter 17: Designing Your Ideal Life

Designing your ideal life involves envisioning your desired future and taking steps to achieve it. It's about creating a life that reflects your values, passions, and goals.

One way to design your ideal life is by setting clear and achievable goals. This involves reflecting on what you truly want in different areas of your life, such as career, relationships, health, and personal growth. By setting specific and actionable goals, you can create a roadmap for achieving your desired future. This chapter discusses the importance of goal-setting and provides a framework for designing a life of simplicity, connection, and abundance.

Another aspect of designing your ideal life is taking consistent action towards your goals. This involves breaking down your goals into smaller, manageable steps and staying committed to your vision. It's important to celebrate your progress and stay motivated. This chapter provides practical tips for staying on track and achieving your ideal life.

Designing a Life of Simplicity, Connection, and Abundance is your guide to creating a fulfilling and intentional life. In today's fast-paced world, it's easy to get caught up in the hustle and lose sight of what truly matters. This book offers a refreshing perspective, showing you how to embrace minimalism, mindfulness, and meaningful connections to live a life of purpose and joy.

Through 17 thoughtfully crafted chapters, you'll explore practical strategies for decluttering your physical space, simplifying your schedule, and nurturing self-care. You'll discover the power of gratitude, the importance of living with intention, and the benefits of financial simplicity. Each chapter is filled with actionable tips and inspiring insights to help you create a life that aligns with your values and aspirations.

From building meaningful relationships to cultivating creativity and embracing change, **Designing a Life of Simplicity, Connection, and Abundance** empowers you to design a life that reflects your true self. Whether you're seeking balance, pursuing your passions, or finding connection in nature, this book provides the tools and guidance to help you achieve a life of abundance and fulfillment.

Join us on this transformative journey and learn how to design a life that is rich in simplicity, connection, and abundance. Your ideal life awaits—let's embark on this adventure together.

www.ingramcontent.com/pod-product-compliance
Lightning Source LLC
LaVergne TN
LVHW010445070526
838199LV00066B/6213